LITTLE RED BOOK

of

READING AND LISTENING SKILLS

Bestsellers by the Author

CATEGORY I

Language skills for all age groups from class 3 onwards: Little Red Book Series

CATEGORY II

For beginners: *A Child's First Dictionary* (Little Red Book Series)

CATEGORY III

To develop a love for reading among schoolchildren and also for adults, a collection of the best stories by renowned writers: Masterpieces of World Fiction series.

CATEGORY IV

For developing quiz instinct and general awareness: The Fun Fact series—*Fun with Numbers, Fun with Riddles,* etc.; *A2Z Quiz Book; The Book of Firsts and Lasts;* the Things You Ought to Know series—*Natural Surroundings* and *Game Time*

CATEGORY V

Motivational books: *The Book of Virtues, The Book of Motivation*

CATEGORY VI

For overall preparation and general awareness: *The Students' Companion*

CATEGORY VII

Teachers' reference book: *A2Z Book of Word Origins, The Ultimate Book of Common Errors*

LITTLE RED BOOK
of
READING AND LISTENING SKILLS

Terry O'Brien

Published by
Rupa Publications India Pvt. Ltd 2016
7/16, Ansari Road, Daryaganj
New Delhi 110002

Sales centres:
Prayagraj Bengaluru Chennai
Hyderabad Jaipur Kathmandu
Kolkata Mumbai

Copyright © Terry O'Brien 2016

The views and opinions expressed in this book are the author's own and the facts are as reported by him/her which have been verified to the extent possible, and the publishers are not in any way liable for the same.

All rights reserved.
No part of this publication may be reproduced, transmitted, or stored in a retrieval system, in any form or by any means, electronic, mechanical, photocopying, recording or otherwise, without the prior permission of the publisher.

P-ISBN: 978-81-291-3987-0
E-ISBN: 978-81-291-3024-2

Fifth impression 2023

10 9 8 7 6 5

The moral right of the author has been asserted.

Typeset by Innovative Processors, New Delhi

Printed in India

This book is sold subject to the condition that it shall not, by way of trade or otherwise, be lent, resold, hired out, or otherwise circulated, without the publisher's prior consent, in any form of binding or cover other than that in which it is published.

Preface

Reading is a skill that one can hone. It is a skill which trains us 'how' to read rather than what to read. Of course, a person is known by the books he reads!

The 3Rs of reading are plain and simple: Read, Record, Recall. Some of us read a book but do not retain what we read. It is for this that one has to train in the skill of reading.

What is Reading?

'Reading' is the means of looking at a series of written symbols and getting meaning from them. When we read, we use our eyes to receive written symbols (letters, punctuation marks and spaces): a physical activity. It is also a cerebral activity: we use our brain to convert these written symbols into words, sentences and paragraphs that communicate something to us. Reading can be silent (in our head) or aloud (so that other people can hear).

Reading is a receptive skill—through it we receive information. But the art of reading also requires the skill of speaking so that we can pronounce the words that we read. Thus reading is also a productive skill; we are both receiving information and transmitting it.

Reading is the third of the four language skills, which are:

- **Listening**
- **Speaking**
- **Reading**
- **Writing**

In our own language, reading is usually the third language skill that we learn.

Now comes the paradoxical question: do we need to read in order to speak English? The short answer is no. Some native speakers cannot read or write but they speak English fluently. On the other hand, reading is something that you can do on your own and that greatly broadens your vocabulary, thus helping you in speaking (and in listening and writing). Reading is therefore a highly valuable skill and activity, and it is recommended that English learners try to read as much as possible in English. Let us ponder over these statements:

- Readers can be divided into two classes: those who read to remember and those who read to forget.

- There are worse crimes than burning books. One of them is not reading them.

- You know you've read a good book when you turn the last page and feel a little as if you have lost a friend.

- 'In a good book, the best is between the lines.'

  —Swedish proverb

- 'Some books leave us free and some books make us free.'

—Ralph Waldo Emerson

So let us make a pledge: let us add spice and meaning in our lives with the skills of reading. So welcome to the joys of reading.

And, of course, hearing is not listening. So listen for better understanding.

Happy Reading!

Terry O'Brien

Reading

READING TIPS

- The fact is that there is no substitute for reading a book.

- Book lovers habitually accumulate more than they can actually read. One usually confuses the purchase of books with the acquisition of their contents.

- Arguments over whether it's better to read, say, Dante's *Inferno* or Dan Brown's *Inferno* will always be with us.

- There is a plethora of free ebooks: pick and choose.

- The old 'no talking' signs in libraries were there for a reason. It's not what we read that matters, it's how.

- Reading is a broad church. But it is still a church. It might behove the congregation to bow its head occasionally in silent contemplation.

THE PEOPLE WHO READ ARE THE PEOPLE WHO LEAD

See the groups at railway bookstalls, the crowds in the bookstores, the large number of young people in the libraries of Kolkata and Chennai. More and more people are reading. Here are a few points to consider:

- The question for more and more people in today's world is not 'Can you read?' but 'Can you read well?'

- Reading walks hand in hand with freedom. Those in bondage are not given books. The more we read, the freer we are. It opens the doors to possibilities, alternatives and options that we could not see before.

- Read what Skinner calls 'the literature of dignity': The great prose and poetry of your culture and others' that depict characters struggling to free themselves from persons and situations that seek to diminish their personal worth.

- Read at least half an hour a day. If the average reader reads thirty minutes a day, he would read forty books a year. Forty great books is one great education.

- Be selective. Four centuries ago, a thousand books were published in a year, today a thousand a day. Some are trash; others, unforgettable experiences. You don't feed rubbish to your body. Don't feed it to your mind.

- Be critical when you read. Reading is thinking with questions. What's the author saying? Do I agree with him? Is his reasoning sound? Give the author your eyes but not your mind.

➤ Talk about your reading. This forces you to digest what you have read and enriches you with another person's reactions.

➤ And, above all, remember: 'A bestseller is the gilded tomb of a mediocre writer'.

THE TIME MACHINE

In the year 2020, when the travel-weary passenger on the moon-shuttle has had his fill of dinner on the anti-gravity magnetic tray, three-dimensional TV, intergalactic weather reports and conversational banter with the space air hostess as she floats by—he'll then settle back in his space-reclining couch and return to that important, private activity each of us does alone: reading. Batman and Superman may well join him then!

The act of reading is essentially a process of thinking. It has further scope than any camera. It will be process on the cosmic screen of your own mind. It is an individual act. It is an involvement. The reader is proactive; he/she makes the printed communication happen, releases the magic, the 'rainbow bridge', the 'only connect' that causes words on a page to leap into living thoughts, ideas, emotions.

And no matter how many millions may be on the receiving end of the message, it is addressed and received by individuals one at a time. This is done in the splendid solitude of his or her own mind. Out comes the truth: 'I am less alone when alone'. It is here that the silent language of print can whisper, rage, implore, accuse, break into a song, explode into revelation, stab the conscience. It takes us to the place where we can hear the 'Abyssinian maid' with her dulcimer, the muse.

Aeschylus knew this when he called written words 'physicians'. And so did Hitler when he burned them. Because mobs roar, but individuals think. They think. They read. And they ask questions that alter the course of the world.

Thus PBUH Prophet Mohammad believed: 'A drop of ink is more sacred than the blood of a martyr'.

READING: RESEARCH AND SCHOLARSHIP

Laboratories and research all over the world race into print with discoveries. They report the most significant new work. The reports are exchanged among some of the laboratories on an almost weekly basis. Thus development is the 'mantra' of the times. In terms of reading to be done, all of this averages to more than 400 pages per week.

Projects 'generate paper faster than results'. This day-to-day work gives one 150 additional pages of reading in an average week.

Reports in branches of science are also published in German, French and Russian. Interestingly, laboratories in Japan publish their most important results in English language journals. English-language summaries of Russian publications are available; even full translations. In all, foreign-language reports add 120 pages a week.

Besides these, there are half a dozen other monthlies and quarterlies in subjects so closely related that one must read with careful attention for the clues they provide for one's own work. Thus the weekly input grows by another 100 pages. Then there is the interest and responsibility felt by most scientists to try to be aware of important work going on in all fields of science.

Check This Out

- How many pages do you read weekly?
- Can you afford to be an inefficient reader?

Training Your Eyes

There are two basic methods for improving your reading.
- The first method stresses the training of the eyes.
- The second method stresses the training of the mind.

Let us begin with eye training.

Eye training means three things:

- ➤ Try increasing your eye-span or the number of words you can grasp in one glance. The printed world lies before your eyes to grasp.

- ➤ Try reducing the number of times your eyes regress, flick back, or re-read.

- ➤ Try getting a more rhythmical and regular way of moving the eyes while reading.

Increasing your eye-span:

- ➤ Try to see more with one glance of your eyes. The great footballer, for example, sees not only the players in front of him but also those far to the left and right. Great readers do the same. Be like 'The Black Pearl': Pele.

- ➤ Instant Comprehension. Think of the way you would read your appreciation letter lying on your teacher's desk. Indeed in one glance you would catch it all. No going back, no word by word; rather, instant comprehension. That's the way we should read.

- ➤ The biggest stumbling block: If we read moving our lips as we read, what happens? This slows our reading to the pace of speaking.

Sample This

Word by word reading is like inch by inch walking. Unfortunately many of us do this since this was the way we learned to read but what is good for the child is disastrous for the adult

Develop a rhythm and read on smartly. Look out for the exercises which will show you how your eye works, how to increase your eye-span, and how to develop greater rhythm and speed in getting meaning from the printed page.

[EXERCISE 1]

READING EYE TO EYE

To understand how the eye does its work, do the following exercise.

It takes a little work to get the light straight, but if you do this once you will understand how your eye works when you are reading. Choose one other person to work with you. Here is what you do:

With an ordinary pin make a pin-hole at the centre of this page. Now have your friend stand facing the light in order to light up his face, especially his eyes. You stand facing your friend and ask him to read this page. Hold the page with the pin-hole at eye level. Try to look through the pin-hole. You will be able to do it after a few attempts. You will see the reader's eyes move along the line with little jerks and stops. At the end of the line you will see his eyes swing back like a typewriter to the beginning of the next line. Count each time the eyes stop in covering one line. What is the average number of stops per line? A good reader makes about three stops per line; a poor reader, six or seven.

Did you see his eyes stopping and starting? These stops and starts are called 'eye fixations'. The movements of the eyes are controlled by six small muscles. These six muscles are at work continually starting and stopping the eyes. When they have to start, and stop many times in every line, they get tired quickly, and we say, 'My eyes are tired.' If they stop only a few times in each line, our reading is quick and the eyes remain fresh.

Did you see his eyes going back, re-reading sometimes? These little backward movements of the eyes from right to left are just as bad and harmful as moving our lips while reading.

REMEMBER

'We are like trees:

> we must create new leaves,

>> new directions;

>>> in order to grow.'

[EXERCISE 2]

DOWN THE PYRAMID

Suppose you had a tin of sweets that you could put your hand in and take out as many as you could in one handful, but one handful only. What would you do? You probably would s-t-r-e-t-c-h your hand and take as many sweets as you could in one grasp!

That is the first thing we should do when we read: <u>grasp as many words as we can in one glance:</u>

Here's a way to make the corners of your eyes work. Develop greedy eyes.

A. Take a postcard and draw a small arrow on the top centre:

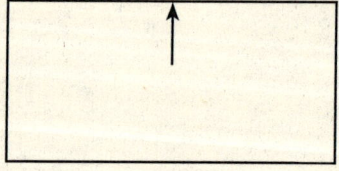

B. Put the card with its arrowhead on top of the arrowhead of one of the word pyramids given below. Fix your eyes sharply on the arrowhead of the card and do not let your eyes move or shift focus. Now

Little Red Book of Reading and Listening Skills 13

draw the card down slowly along the vertical line. Do not move your eyes. How far down can you go before you fail to see all the words in the line? Don't let your eyes shift or lose focus. Steady. No cheating. Stretch your eyes. Practise this every day for five minutes. Keep records. The numbers on the side, tell you in type units how large an eye-span you have at this time. How wide is your eye-span now?

Doing this for five or ten minutes a day will improve your eye-span. You should be able to get up to thirty at least with practice. This has two effects: less work for the eye muscles and more food for your mind.

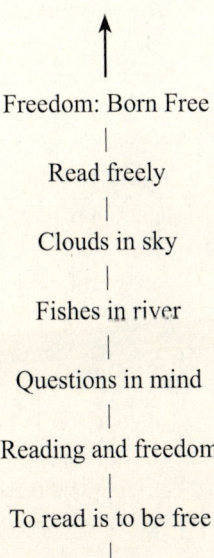

Freedom: Born Free
|
Read freely
|
Clouds in sky
|
Fishes in river
|
Questions in mind
|
Reading and freedom
|
To read is to be free
|

Slaves can't read books
|
Reading frees men's minds
|
Ignorance makes men captive
|
Ignorance chains a man's mind
|
Knowledge liberates men's minds
|
Question
|
Think hard
|
Seek meaning
|
Teach yourself
|
Educate yourself
|
Talk about reading
|
Read great books
|
Increase your learning
|
Increase your vocabulary
|
Concentration is the thing
|

Little Red Book of Reading and Listening Skills

Look for the flow of thought
|
Concentrate all your attention
↑
Read on
|
Big jumps
|
Greedy eyes
|
Don't go back
|
Don't move lips
|
Catch the meaning
|
Reading is thinking
|
Watch first sentences
|
Watch out for keywords
|
One thought, one paragraph
|
Grasp quickly central ideas
|
Scan all headings and italics
|
Increase your general knowledge

|
Catch the meaning: that's the game
|
Read daily
|
Remain alert
|
Read for half an hour
|
Read as you ride
|
Search for meaning
|
Meaning is the thing
|
Only meaning satisfies
|
Mind is made for meaning
|
Read last paragraphs first
|
Always note words in italics
|
Meaning is what really matters
|
Read for at least half an hour a day
|
Mind lives on meaning not on words

[EXERCISE 3]

RAPID RHYTHMIC READING

Here's another toning practice. Read the following several times. Each time try to read it a little faster, but without losing any meaning. You will need a watch for this exercise. Try to do it smoothly, grasping a whole phrase with each glance or fixation of the eye, and only three fixations per line. All right, check the time and start.

The secret	of reading	lies in
thinking with questions.	To read	is to think
with questions.	We try	to follow
the writer's thought	but also	many questions
must dance	in our heads.	Is this true?
Do I agree?	What follows?	Where next?
Such questions	must be	in our heads
as we read.		
With regular practice	we can increase	our eye-span.
Our eyes move	by stops and starts	across the page.
These fixations	or glances	are important

in reading. You should try to grasp as many words as you can in one fixation. Grasping many words in one fixation is very helpful to both the mind and the eye. The mind gets more meaning and the eye has less work. When you read word-by-word the mind gets less meaning and also the muscles of the eye become tired. Three stops or fixations to a line is sufficient. So remember the less stops for the eyes the better for the mind. Do this exercise every day for five minutes each time trying to increase your speed as you read. You will need a watch to keep time but push yourself faster and faster along the lines but of course without any loss of meaning. There should be a rhythm in the movement of your eyes. You can become, if you will, a skilled reader, a thinking reader, a faster reader, an intelligent reader. It all depends on your determination to practise.

Theory without practice is sterile. Practice without theory is blind. Resolve today to become skilled in the art of reading. Do this exercise for five minutes every day before picking up your regular reading. The rhythm will carry over from this exercise to the other.

You have finished. See the time. Write it down.

Seconds

1. _____
2. _____
3. _____
4. _____
5. _____
6. _____
7. _____
8. _____
9. _____
10. _____

Average time _____

Remember: Go a little faster than what is comfortable, and keep trying to increase the speed.

[EXERCISE 4]

MAKE YOUR READING MACHINE

You don't have to import a reading machine. You can make your own.

Here's how to make your own reading machine. It's practically as good as any other.

Take a sheet of thick, white paper. About 7 mm from the top, cut out a 3 cm window. The window should be wide enough to extend 1 cm beyond the side of the columns of the print on the page of the book with which you will practise. In an ordinary book such a window will frame five or six lines of print. Place the line which you will first read in the middle of the frame. Now begin to read. As you read, begin to pull the piece of paper towards you, moving the frame down over the page. The lines which you have read will disappear above and new lines will appear at the bottom. Be sure you pull the sheet with a steady pace. Maintain a steady pull, keep up the pressure.

That isn't CRICKET my friend

Cricket has been described to an alien in the following way:

'Cricket is quite simple. You have two sides: ours and theirs. One out in the field and one in. Each man in the side that is in goes out, and when he's out he comes in, and the next man goes in until he is out. Then, when they have all been in and are all out, the side that has been out in the field comes in, and the side that has been in goes out and tries to get out those coming in. Sometimes there are still men in and not out. Then when both sides have been in and out, including not outs, that's the end of the game. It's really very simple, although sometimes it has some people confused.'

That short paragraph describes cricket but it also tells you a lot about reading. If you are very familiar with cricket, then you had no trouble understanding it. If you are not familiar with cricket, then you probably had considerable difficulty and confusion. Among other things, it shows:

> Familiarity with the subject matter makes a big difference in the speed of comprehension.

> There's more to reading than merely increasing the eye-span.

> You need a flexible strategy to become a really efficient reader.

In the effort to become an efficient reader, eye training is important. But even more important is mind training or developing a strategy for getting the meaning from a page of print.

'All that mankind has done, thought, gained is lying as a magic preservation in the pages of books.'

BE A STRATEGIC READER

Eye training is important; mind training is even more important. The truth is that if you learn to use your mind better while reading, the eyes will take care of themselves.

So if you really want to become an intelligent and efficient reader, you must adopt a strategy. A strategic reader is a reader with a system for getting the meaning out of his reading.

Think of two football teams. They have a strategy. They don't just rush out and play against their opponents. They have done much work even before the game begins. They study their opponents. The goalkeeper—does he move equally well to the left and right? Does he make the first move when he is attacked alone? Or does he wait for the striker to move first? The centre-forward—where does he usually pass? What are the weak spots of the defence? Which players tire out in the second half? The team wins championships because they play intelligently. They approach a football game systematically.

Many persons, otherwise very intelligent, are very poor readers. They have no plan of attack, no system. The whole secret of reading, however, lies in one small phrase. The magic phrase is: Survey Q3R. Adopt this system and you will win in the game of getting meaning from a page of print.

5 Pillars Of Effective Readers

Survey	S
Restate	Q
Review	R
Question	R
React	R

First Step: Survey

Survey means to get an overview, the overall picture before going into details. Reading without first surveying is like going on a journey without a map, or jumping on a bus without knowing where it's going. Here's how to Survey:

A. In the case of a book, first read the Preface, Contents, and Summaries at the end of the chapters. Figure out the author's purpose and audience. Skim through the rest.

B. In the case of a chapter or article:

➢ Read the first and last sentences of the first and last paragraphs and the first sentence of every paragraph in between. The first and last paragraphs of any chapter are likely to be more important than the other paragraphs, just as the first sentence of every paragraph is usually more important than the other sentences. In reading these sentences, you are usually reading the most meaningful sentences in the article. This can often give you the entire thought of the article within a minute or two. A summary paragraph is particularly important.

- Notice the paragraph size. Long paragraphs usually mean loaded (developed ideas); short paragraphs, easygoing ideas (a series of underdeveloped thoughts).

- Words in italics. The author puts something in italics just to say to you that this is something he/she wishes to stress. This is important.

- Graphs, diagrams, tables. The author feels he can express his point more clearly through these than through words.

- Keywords. In every paragraph there are a few words which unlock the meaning. Note also signpost words like first, secondly, in summary, in short.

- Skim with your finger. In ten to fifteen seconds, in the form of S-shapes or waves, run your finger down the page.

(Time to be spent in Surveying: 5 per cent of total time.)

Exercise: Two Lightning Surveys

You can do these exercises alone or with a friend.

> - Select a fairly serious book. You have thirty seconds. Within that time find the exact purpose and specific audience that the author has in mind. Check the answer for accuracy: do you really know where the author's going? Where he's taking you?

> - Select a chapter of the book. You have two minutes. Read the first and last sentences of the first and last paragraphs and the first sentence of every paragraph in between. When the two minutes have elapsed, close the book and tell your partner or recite aloud as much as you can of the main points of the material.

Question

After surveying the material, you're still not ready to read. Never start reading until you have questions in your head. You should be asking questions before you start reading, as well as while you are reading. Questions should start with the title: what does the title tell me about the contents of the article or the book? What do I think will be included and what do I think will be excluded? How much time do I wish to devote to this reading?

Let us take an example. Suppose the title is 'Great Batsmen of India', The title itself gives you many clues as to what will be in the material and what will not. You know it will be about batsmen and not about bowlers. You know it will be about leading cricket batsmen, not mediocre ones; and you know it will be about batsmen in India and not about those in other countries. You try to think about how much you already know about the great batsmen of India. You may wonder whether Gavaskar's name will be included or Tendulkar's.

Reading is thinking plus asking questions. We only learn when we ask questions; we read and remember best when we read to answer our questions and problems. By raising questions in our mind continually from the title and headings, we get in the proper mental position for reading.

We must ask questions not only before we read but while we read. Just like a person driving a motorbike. He has to drive defensively: will that cyclist turn left or will he continue straight? Will that stray dog dash across the road or won't it? The careful driver is always asking questions. So, too, as we read, we should ask questions. Do I agree? Who says so? What proof? What follows from this? Where will the author go from here? Questions should continually reverberate in our minds as we read. Otherwise we will be doing nothing but just watching a book.

(Time to be spent on Questions: 5 per cent of the total time.)

EXERCISE: QUESTION

Let us suppose that you wanted to read Khushwant Singh's *Train to Pakistan*. Consider only the title. What would you guess are the answers to these questions?

1. Which neighbours will he be discussing?
2. Could it be a a historical novel?
3. Will it recount the Partition of India in August 1947?
4. Instead of depicting the Partition will it deal with the social fabric then?

Putting questions in your head before you start makes you read with a purpose.

THIRD STEP: READ

Let's see now. You've picked a place where as far as possible you won't be disturbed, and where there is as little noise as possible. You know where the author is going, and you have questions churning in your head. You're ready to read. So read!

Read as you ride a cycle; slowly uphill, quickly downhill, and carefully where there is danger. Read difficult matter slowly, light matter quickly, and tendentious matter cautiously. Be flexible.

Keep a steady pressure on yourself to move as quickly as possible. Just as in cycling, so in reading, we pay more attention when we're moving quickly than when we go slowly. The fast road driver is usually the fast learner.

Read for thought-units not word-units. You receive nothing for merely reading words. Words don't fill the mind but meaning does. Your mind doesn't live on words;

what matters is meaning. So keep looking for answers to questions as you read.

Read actively. If your mind is not working, you're not reading. You're probably only looking at a book. Reading is thinking with questions. Look for the main thoughts and important details. Sometimes under a deluge of words, there's only a single idea.

Every hour give yourself a break. Get up, stretch. Look outside the window.

(Time to be spent in Reading: 50 per cent of total time.)

REDUCING EXERCISE

Read the following letter. It has 116 words. See how many words can be omitted without loss of meaning.

Mr Jatin Mehra

The Students' Book Agency
Daryaganj
DELHI.

Dear Mr Mehra,

We have received your letter dated 12 February, in which you have asked for a copy of our publication: *A2Z Quiz Book*. We were very happy to receive your letter and shall be happy also to render you any service.

We regret to inform you that *A2Z Quiz Book* is currently

out of stock. The demand for this book has been so great that we could not keep up with the demand.

We will, however, publish a reprint of that publication within the next six months since the response to it has been very favourable. When the new reprint is ready we will inform you to find out whether you still wish to place an order.

Yours faithfully,

A.K. Singh
Sales in-charge

In how few words can you express the real meaning of each of the paragraphs? You can do it in less than twenty words for all three.

1st paragraph: _____

2nd paragraph: _____

3rd paragraph: _____

FOURTH STEP: RESTATE

To restate means to put your book down at intervals and to tell yourself what you have read. It's the key to rock solid learning. Good readers do it. Poor readers do not.

Regularly, then, stop reading, look up and tell yourself the main points and important details of what you are reading. It can be a little embarrassing but it's the only way to see what you remember.

When should you restate? Every paragraph would be too much but a chapter may be too long. If the reading has headings, restating at the end of every heading may be a good interval.

Research has shown that generally the reader who restates can remember three times more than one who does not.

What's your purpose in reading? To watch a book or to learn?

If it's learning, make it a habit of restating.

(Time to be spent on Restating: 30 per cent of total time.)

TRYST WITH DESTINY

('Tryst with Destiny' was a speech delivered by Jawaharlal Nehru, the first Prime Minister of independent India, to the Indian Constituent Assembly in the Parliament on the eve of India's Independence, on 15 August 1947.)

'Long years ago, we made a tryst with destiny, and now the time comes when we shall redeem our pledge, not wholly or in full measure, but very substantially. At the stroke of the midnight hour, when the world sleeps, India will awake to life and freedom. A moment comes, which comes but rarely in history, when we step out from the old to the new, when an age ends, and when the soul of a nation, long suppressed, finds utterance. It is fitting that at this solemn moment we take the pledge of dedication to the service of India and her people and to the still larger cause of humanity.

'At the dawn of history India started on her unending quest, and trackless centuries are filled with her striving and the grandeur of her successes and her failures. Through good and ill fortune alike she has never lost sight of that quest or forgotten the ideals which gave her strength. We end today a period of ill fortune and India discovers herself again. The achievement we celebrate today is but a step, an opening of opportunity to the greater triumphs and achievements that await us. Are we brave enough and wise enough to grasp this opportunity and accept the challenge of the future?

'Freedom and power bring responsibility. The responsibility rests upon this Assembly, a sovereign body representing the sovereign people of India. Before the birth of freedom, we have endured all the pains of labour and our hearts are heavy with the memory of this sorrow. Some of those pains continue even now. Nevertheless, the past is over and it is the future that beckons to us now. That future is not one of ease or resting but of incessant striving so that we might fulfill the pledges we have so often taken and the one we shall take today. The service of India means the service of the millions who suffer. It means the ending of poverty and ignorance and disease and inequality of opportunity. The ambition of the greatest man of our generation has been to wipe every tear from every eye. That may be beyond us but as long as there are tears and suffering, so long our work will not be over.

'And so we have to labour and to work and work hard to give reality to our dreams. Those dreams are for India, but they are also for the world, for all the nations and peoples are too closely knit together today for anyone of them to imagine that it can live apart.

'Peace has been said to be indivisible; so is freedom, so is prosperity now, and so also is disaster in this one world that can no longer be split into isolated fragments. To the people of India, whose representatives we are, we appeal to join us with faith and confidence in this great adventure. This is no time for petty and destructive criticism, no time for ill-will or blaming others. We have to build the noble mansion of free India where all her children may dwell.'

RESTATE EXERCISE

Turn the piece over and restate aloud as much of it as you can. Then give it to a friend to read, but do not have him or her restate. A week or two later, ask your friend what he or she can recall. Who remembers more? Is it your friend or you?

Fifth Step: Review

Review, the fifth and last step in your reading strategy, is simply repeating the first four steps. You again survey, question, read, and restate, and now not what you will read but what you have read.

So to review, skim back over the material, surveying the headings again, answering your questions and the questions they pose, rereading items you are unsure about or can't remember, and restating the central message with its parts and their relation.

The time to review is right after you read. It's reviewing that gives you that 'I've got it' feeling and also the confidence and satisfaction.

Some people don't review. They bore on through a book like white ants, on and on, never looking back, getting lost, tired and discouraged. 'Two hours' reading and I can't remember a thing,' they'd say.

Reviewing is like marking your own examination paper. Skimming back over the matter, you can see whether you deserve a first class, third, or fail. You may rate yourself low on your first attempts but very soon you'll see your grades shoot up.

(Time to be spent on Reviewing: 10 per cent of the total time.)

Exercise: Review

> Turn this book over now and restate as many tips for better reading as have been suggested so far.

> Now review the pages on reading. Check to see what percentage of the important points you remember.

100 per cent   75 per cent   50 per cent   25 per cent

How to Read a Newspaper

Recent events in India and abroad have once again underlined the crucial role of newspapers in a democratic society. Democracy cannot survive unless citizens can view developments and problems with objectivity and reason. For this they need continual access to an accurate and full answer to the question: 'What's new?'

Despite shortages of paper and finance, the country is blessed with some excellent newspapers, brilliant analysts, courageous editors, indefatigable reporters, perceptive photographers, and delightful cartoonists.

Here's one system for getting more from the daily of your choice:

> Scan headlines   2 minutes
> (Good opportunity to practise skimming)
> This gives you the overall view

- ➤ Read the big news stories of the day   6 minutes
  (local, national, international)
  This keeps you informed

- ➤ Read the editorials   6 minutes
  This tells you what events mean
  (at least as the editor sees it)

- ➤ Look at the cartoons and photographs   1 minute
  This for insight, humour, and keen observation.
  (R.K. Laxman was a great sensitive cartoonist)

- ➤ Read what you like   5 minutes
  (Sports, films, comics, etc.)
  This is for fun and relaxation

NOTE: It is difficult to get the news from poems.

READING THE NEWSPAPER CRITICALLY

When a person stands before a work of art, what is being judged: the work of art or the observer?

An examination: does it reveal more about the student or the teacher who developed it? Much the same is the situation of a reporter before the news event.

Here is a note by a writer about a certain famous statesman:

> *'I only know him as far as I know him; and that fully depends as much upon who I am as it does upon who he is.'*

Let us distinguish between mature reporter and mature reporting.

The newspaper reporter or editor like us sees the world, its events and ideas through the prism of their attitudes. No wonder, then, that viewpoints, values and biases are sometimes thinly veiled. Try as they may to see things objectively, they can never see things with any eyes other than their own.

Yet not only reporters and editors but headlines and layout editors are influential too. How they summarize a story in a few words and choose the position and page to display it are very important, for most people read only the headlines and the sub-headlines and these on some pages and in some places more than others.

An Exercise and a Question

Read through a newspaper, examining the headlines and sub-headings. See whether you can find a headline of any story that is inappropriate, inaccurate or misleading.

Do you have any comment on the following terms? 'Antisocial elements', 'troublemakers', 'terrorists', 'freedom fighters', 'loyal workers', 'unruly elements', 'interference in domestic affairs', 'radicals', 'fanatical', 'reactionary', 'conservative', 'progressive', and 'tyranny of the unelected'.

CAN THE PRESS TELL THE TRUTH?

Posing this question, D. McDonald, editor and journalist, answers it by saying that a 'substantially truthful account of contemporary public affairs' is possible but the difficulties he lists are good for us as newspaper readers to note.

> - The reporter can only capture events through his or her uniquely conditioned eyes and ears.

> - What is news? Are ideas news or only particular events? Are contexts and trends news?

> - The same words have differrent meanings for different people.

> - Events are complex and open-ended yet the pressure on reporters is for the sensational, clear and complete.

> - The sources of news dry up for the reporter who does not 'cooperate'.

> - Some newspapers give a higher primacy to profit than others; all must pay their bills.

> - The event may be factually reported but only the context, origins, and developments can tell its meaning.

> Some newspapers use only a small piece of the copy they get daily. Who selects it? On what basis or values have they been selected?

> Interpretation is dependent on the maturity of the observer; immature observer, immature interpretation.

> The recent, the novel, the conflict get an emphasis disproportionate to their importance.

An Exercise and a Question

List the news items appearing on the front page of your newspaper today. Do this every day for a week. Then analyse the list. Were there many new stories? How many stories stayed on the front page and for how long? What does this tell you about 'what is news'?

'Ideas are news, and we are not covering the news of the mind as we should. This is where rebellion, revolution, and war start, but we minimize the conflict of ideas and emphasize the conflict in the streets without relating the second to the first.' Do you agree?

Reading Goal

In the box below, write in one goal that you would like to achieve in your reading. Write the goal in measurable, realistic and time-bound terms.

For example: 'I want to read about Gandhi.' That is not a goal.

'I want to read Gandhi's *The Story of My Experiments with Truth* by the end of this year.' That is a goal because it is measurable and time-bound.

After writing the goal, assess it for Importance (I) and Difficulty (D). Use the symbols H for high, M for medium, and L for low. Also check to see whether there is any conflict with any other goal of yours (C).

Reading goal for the next six months: I D C

In a very real sense people who have read good literature have lived more than people who cannot or will not read. It is not true that we have only one life to live; if we can read, we can live as many more lives and as many kinds of lives as we wish.

Fast-Track Questions

> How many languages are printed on every Indian currency note? What languages are they? In what order do they appear? What language appears on Indian currency notes which does not appear in the 8th schedule of the Indian Constitution?

> Name three animals whose images are found on every Indian currency note.

> The Governor of the Reserve Bank of India is the only person with his signature on Indian paper currency. True or false?

> How many lions are sitting back to back in the state emblem of India?

> What is the length in centimetres of the diameter of a ten rupee coin? Guess at closest figure.

   (a) 1 (b) 2 (c) 1.5
   (d) 3 (e) 2.5

> What is the length in centimetres of the diameter of a new 50 paise coin?

   (a) 2.5 (b) 4 (c) 2
   (d) 3 (e) 23 mm

> Which way does a CD turn: clockwise or counter-clockwise?

> When you walk normally, do your arms swing with or against the rhythm of your legs?

Indeed deep or repeated reading should be well-integrated into the curriculum.

Catch the habit early.

How Poems for Kids Boost Reading Skills—1. It rhymes (mostly!)

> Rhyming language can help struggling kids read more smoothly.

Little Red Book of Reading and Listening Skills

- Rhymes also show kids that words are made up of syllables, which helps them recognize the same sound in different words. Plus, it can improve spelling—it's not so far from 'cat' to 'mat,' once you have the 'at.'

- It develops vocabulary.

- Poetry incorporates words kids don't usually encounter, yet the form's short.

- It introduces literary concepts.

- Even silly nursery rhymes use alliteration, metaphors, and similes.

- It's easy and fun to memorize.

- Memorization helps kids internalize patterns of language.

- When they recite, they learn how to enunciate as well as to pronounce unfamiliar words.

OPEN A BOOK AND YOU WILL FIND

PEOPLE AND PLACES OF EVERY KIND

OPEN A BOOK

AND YOU CAN BE

ANYTHING YOU WANT TO BE

Reading Develops

Learning to read as a child usually helps in the ability to read simple material relatively easily.

Gradually, we are introduced to new vocabulary and more complex sentence structures. Early school textbooks offer us facts or 'truths' about the world which we are required to learn; we are not, at this stage, encouraged to question the authority of the writers of these published materials.

As schooling progresses, however, we are led to consider a range of perspectives or ways of looking at a topic rather than just one. We learn to compare these perspectives and begin to form opinions about them.

This change in reading from basics (gathering facts) to a deep approach (interpreting) is essential in order to gain the most out of our studies.

Reading becomes not simply a way to see what is said but to recognize and interpret what is said.

The Goal of Reading

- Most of us read in everyday life for different purposes. You are reading this page now for a purpose.
- We read to gain factual information for practical use, for example, a train timetable or a cinema listing. In this case we rarely need to analyse or interpret.

- We may also read fiction in order to be entertained; but as part of an English Literature degree, we analyse the author's writing style, motives etc.
- Many of us read newspapers and magazines, either in print or online, to inform us about current events.
- When reading textbooks you should be always reading to interpret and analyse. Nothing should be taken as fact or 'truth'. You will be engaged in, what is termed critical reading.

ATTITUDES TO READING

Perseverance

Often, when we begin to read books related to a new topic, we find that the language and style are difficult to follow.

This can be off-putting and disheartening, but persevere; specialist subject areas will contain their own specialist 'language' which you will need to learn. Perseverance will help you understand the vocabulary or jargon associated with the specific subject area.

Use a Dictionary

- A useful aid to reading is to have a good quality dictionary.
- A specialist dictionary is necessary for specific subjects.
- You may use an online dictionary.

NOTE: Even though a dictionary can be useful, it should not be relied upon too heavily. Dictionaries do not often take into account the context.

ACTIVE READING: COMPREHENSION AND RATE

Students frequently remark that they don't have enough time to read through all of their assignments during the week. However, many students have bad habits and subscribe to irresponsible reading.

Some Common Reading Fallacies

- Read every word.
- One reading is sufficient.
- Don't skip passages.
- Machines improve speed.
- A faster rate means less comprehension.

CRACK THE READING MYTHS

MYTH 1: I have to read every word.

MYTH 2: Reading once is enough.

MYTH 3: It is wrong to skip passages while reading.

MYTH 4: Machines are necessary to improve reading speed.

MYTH 5: If I skim or read too rapidly my comprehension will drop.

MYTH 6: There is something about my eyes that keeps me from reading fast.

STEPS TO FOLLOW IN SKIMMING FOR THE MAIN IDEAS

1. First, read the title of the chapter or selection carefully. Determine what clues it gives you as to what the selection is about. Watch for keywords like 'causes,' 'results,' 'effects,' etc., and do not overlook signal words such as those suggesting controversy (e.g., 'versus,' 'pros and cons'), which indicate that the author is planning to present both sides of an argument.

2. Look carefully at the headings and other relative clues. These tip you off to the main points that the author wants you to learn.

3 Rs FOR READING EFFECTIVELY

READ: Read the chapter paragraph by paragraph. Read and re-read until you can answer the question: 'What did the author say in this paragraph?'

RECORD: Once you are able to **describe** what is in the paragraph, you will want to retain that learning by

underlining, making notes in the margin, or **making notes in your notebook.**

RECITE (RECALL): Cover up your notes or printed page and **recite** aloud. Remember: try and try again, until you can say it.

APPLY SQ3R METHOD FOR THOROUGH STUDY

Step 1: SURVEY

Look over the material critically. Skim through the book and read topical and sub-topical headings and sentences. Read the summaries at the end of chapters and books. Try to anticipate what the author is going to say.

Read with a pencil: WRITE these notes on paper, in sequence; then look over the jottings to get an overall idea or picture. This will enable you to see where you are going.

Step 2: QUESTIONS

Instead of reading paragraph headings such as 'Basic Concepts of Reading', change to read, 'What are the Basic Concepts of Reading?'

WRITE these questions out. Look at the questions to see the emphasis and direction; then attempt to give plausible answers before reading further.

Step 3: READ

Read with smoothness and alertness to answer the questions. Use all the techniques and principles demonstrated in class.

WRITE notes in your own words under each question. Take a minimum number of notes and use these notes as a skeleton.

Step 4: RECALL

Without looking at your book or notes, mentally visualize and sketch in your own words the high points of the material immediately upon completing the reading.

- ➢ This forces you to check understanding.
- ➢ This channels the material into a natural and usable form.
- ➢ This points up what you do not understand.
- ➢ This forces you to think.

Step 5: REVIEW

Look at your questions, answers, notes and book to see how well you did recall. Observe carefully the points stated incorrectly or omitted. Fix carefully in mind the logical sequence of the entire idea, concepts, or problem. Finish up with a mental picture of the WHOLE.

USING YOUR TEXTBOOK

When you purchase a new book, there are several things you should do automatically.

I. Look in the **front**:

- **Read** and think about the table of contents.

- This will show you the overall organization of the course and help identify what's important.

- It will get you interested in the material.

- Glance over any preface or foreword to see what the book is about.

- Consider the title. This is often a significant statement about the book's 'angle.' Do you know the author?

II. Look in the **back**:

A. Glance at the index. This is a listing of subjects and the pages on which they can be found.

- You can tell from the percentage of known and unknown words how difficult the text will be for you.

- You can see with great precision what the course is concerned with.

- You can look up specific items of interest.

- As a review for tests, you can easily look up unknown items since the page number is given.

B. Is there a glossary listing unknown words and their definitions?

- The main concern of many courses is to teach the vocabulary of the subject. This is a vital section, not something to be ignored.

- Make a page tab out of scotch tape, and undertake to study and learn these words during the term.

C. Determine what other possibly useful materials are in the back **before** you need them. You don't have to read them now; just know that they exist.

III. Determine how a typical chapter is constructed. Structure your approach accordingly.

IV. Don't be afraid to write in your book: vocabulary words, condensations of ideas, personal reactions, etc. Interact with the book the way you'd interact with a person. Your texts provide a valuable resource.

READ WITH A PURPOSE

Always read with a purpose in mind. Before you begin, you should have an idea of why you are reading and what you are looking for or what you want to achieve. Are you reading:

- to locate specific information?
- to understand difficult ideas?
- to gain an overview of something?

- to enjoy words and descriptions (as in poetry or prose)?
- to relax and escape into a novel?

Be Selective About What You Read

- Establish which readings are required for your particular course and which are suggested (not compulsory).
- There will be times when you will need to read an entire article or chapter in detail.

How to Select?

- Know what you are looking for (i.e., have a purpose).
- Identify keywords to help you search.
- Look for these keywords when browsing the table of contents and index of a book for relevant pages.
- Obtain an overview to further narrow down the 'possibly useful' field.

Focus on the Question / Task

- Identify questions you want to answer; actively look for those answers and evidence to inform them.
- Identify a few topic keywords to look for.

Your assignment questions usually have these.

➢ If you are reading for a specific assignment, read with a copy of the question/ task on hand so you don't waste time reading irrelevant material.

BEFORE YOU READ, ESTABLISH WHAT YOU ALREADY KNOW

➢ Ask yourself what you already know or think about this topic.

➢ If you have a reading list, select a source that might offer a good starting point.

➢ Read any related questions to the reading before doing the reading; they may be questions at the back of the chapter or the essay/assignment question.

➢ Identify your expectations: what do you think it will be about?

➢ Ask yourself questions about the topic. Change the title, headings, and sub-headings into questions or ask yourself what you want to find out

NOTE: You will remember more if you read with questions in your mind, rather than adopting the 'sponge' approach: simply trying to absorb everything.

KEEP TRACK OF WHAT YOU READ

Always note where information and ideas come from.

Record details of author, title, place of publication, publisher and date so that you can find the text again if necessary. Always record page numbers with any notes you take.

EFFECTIVE NOTE-MAKING FROM WRITTEN TEXT

It is essential to develop effective note-making skills to ensure that you get the most out of the time that you spend reading.

Jotting down notes in the margins and/or highlighting important sections can also to help you to better understand a text.

Good note-making can also help you to keep a record of what you have read and also to locate information. There is nothing worse than having to spend time tracking down information that you have previously read and now require for an assignment.

THINK ABOUT WHAT YOU WANT TO KNOW

Before you start reading anything, ask yourself why you're reading it. Are you reading with a purpose, or just for pleasure? What do you want to know after you've read it?

Once you know your purpose you can examine the resource to see whether it's going to help you.

STRATEGIES FOR DEVELOPING READING SKILLS

Strategies that can help students read more quickly and effectively:

- ➤ **Previewing:** reviewing titles, section headings, and photo captions to get a sense of the structure and content of a reading selection.
- ➤ **Predicting:** using knowledge of the subject matter to make predictions about content and vocabulary and check comprehension.
- ➤ **Skimming and scanning:** using a quick survey of the text to get the main idea.
- ➤ **Paraphrasing:** stopping at the end of a section to check comprehension by restating the information and ideas in the text.

READING TO LEARN

Reading is an essential part of language instruction at every level because it supports learning in multiple ways.

Reading to learn the language: Reading material is language input.

Reading is for content information.

When students have access to newspapers, magazines, and websites, they are exposed to culture in all its variety.

READING IS THE BEST HOBBY

- Helps you forget about your daily routine. Breaks your monotony.
- You can learn about different cultures, people and places.
- Helps develop your imagination and creativity.
- Comes for free.
- Makes you smart.
- You have topics of discussion.
- Inspires.
- It improves your writing.
- Improves your grammar and vocabulary.
- Improves your communication skills.
- Reading is a versatile form of entertainment: you can do it anywhere.
- Reading expands beyond books such as newspapers, blogs, and online articles.
- Reading is fun, relaxing, funny, exciting, thrilling and much more.
- A mood lifter.
- Self-improvement.
- Improves understanding.
- You get to read other people's minds.
- Boosts your self-esteem.

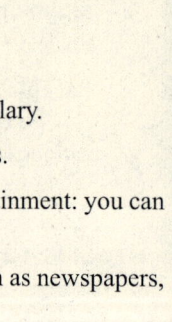

A book is a dream that you hold in your hand.
—Neil Gaiman

Whenever you read a good book, somewhere in the world a door opens to allow in more light.
—Vera Nazarian

Anyone who says they have only one life to live must not know how to read a book.
—Author Unknown

I think of life as a good book. The further you get into it, the more it begins to make sense.
—Harold Kushner

If you only read the books that everyone else is reading, you can only think what everyone else is thinking.
—Haruki Murakami

There are many little ways to enlarge your child's world. Love of books is the best of all.
—Jacqueline Kennedy Onassis

Any book that helps a child to form a habit of reading, to make reading one of his deep and continuing needs, is good for him.
—Maya Angelou

The book you don't read won't help.
—Jim Rohn

Great books help you understand, and they help you feel understood.
—John Green

A good novel tells us the truth about its hero; but a bad novel tells us the truth about its author.

—Gilbert K. Chesterton

In a good book the best is between the lines.

—Swedish Proverb

There are perhaps no days of our childhood we lived so fully as those we spent with a favourite book.

—Marcel Proust

If one cannot enjoy reading a book over and over again, there is no use in reading it at all.

—Oscar Wilde

Read the best books first, or you may not have a chance to read them at all.

—Henry David Thoreau

Reading a book is like rewriting it for yourself.

—Angela Carter

There's nothing wrong with reading a book you love over and over.

—Gail Carson Levine

It is a good rule after reading a new book, never to allow yourself another new one till you have read an old one in between.

—C.S. Lewis

Where is human nature so weak as in the bookstore?

—Henry Ward Beecher

A great book should leave you with many experiences, and slightly exhausted at the end. You live several lives while reading.
—William Styron

One always has a better book in one's mind than one can manage to get onto paper.
—Michael Cunningham

I divide all readers into two classes: those who read to remember and those who read to forget.
—William Lyon Phelps

A book is a device to ignite the imagination.
—Alan Bennett

The most successful people in the world make time to read, study, and learn far beyond. In turn, they're better thinkers, innovators, and leaders.

We can challenge ourselves to read one book a day.

Some Tips for Starting and Finishing a Book a Day, Every Day

- Try an audiobook.
- There are many scenarios where audiobooks are the best: while cleaning the house or exercising.
- Alternate between genres.
- Always carry your book with you.

NOTE: these days it's easy to turn to your smartphone to pass the time, but you're likely to get more long-term benefits from reading a book than your Facebook newsfeed.

Whether you prefer your books on an e-reader or you like them in physical form, carrying them with you always can be the reminder you need to read often. When it's sitting in your bag it's easy to reach on the subway, train, or even during the lunch hour.

Bonus: Learn to speed read.

Listening

LISTENING SKILLS

HOW IMPORTANT IS LISTENING

Two little boys wanted to find out the secret of wisdom. So they decided to go up the mountain, where a wise hermit lived.

One of them asked the master, 'Sir, what is the key to wisdom?' The wise man replied '<u>Listen,</u> my son.' He then fell silent.

The two boys waited eagerly to collect the gems of wisdom. After a long pause one of them asked the teacher again, 'Master, we are listening. Please continue.'

The sage smile and said, 'There is nothing else to be said.'

Indeed, one needs a lot of courage to speak but one needs even greater courage to sit down and listen.

Is Anyone Listening?

When people talk, listen completely. Most people never listen.

—Ernest Hemingway

Most people do not listen with the intent to understand; they listen with the intent to reply.

—Stephen R. Covey

We have two ears and one mouth, so we should listen more than we say.

—Zeno of Citium

Remember the Lord Ganesh syndrome: The ears are the largest!

Remember that you have two ears and one mouth for a reason. This means that you should be listening more than you are talking. It is more beneficial to listen than it is to talk.

How Well Do You Listen?

Healthy listening requires more than just hearing the words.

Listening for Understanding

Checklist:

➢ Listen without judgment or drawing conclusions

before you have all the information.

- Recognize what situations call for selective listening and what situations would benefit from compassionate listening.
- Evaluate the verbal messages as well as body language; note conflicting messages.
- Stay attuned with active listening using full eye contact.
- Don't be afraid to show some emotion in response to what is being said.
- Ask for feedback from the speaker about whether or not you understand what they have communicated.
- Note what information is left out.

How to Be a Good Listener

- Being a good listener can help you to see the world through the eyes of others.
- It enriches your understanding and expands your capacity for empathy.
- It also increases your contact with the outside world by helping you improve your communication skills.
- Good listening skills can provide you with a deeper level of understanding about someone's situation, and helps you to know what words are best to use or which words to avoid.

> As simple as listening (and acknowledging) may seem, doing it well, particularly when disagreements arise, takes sincere effort and lots of practice. If you want to know how to be a good listener, read on to get started.

LISTENING IS NOT THE SAME AS HEARING

Hearing
Sounds that you hear.
Passive process like breathing.
We do it without thinking.

Listening
Focus.
The story—how it is told.
Both verbal and non-verbal messages.

> Listening is a learnt skill and an active process.
> Understanding is the goal of listening.

GENERAL LISTENING TYPES

> **Discriminative Listening:** Develops at an early age in the mother's womb when a baby begins to distinguish between the father's and mother's voice. Basic listening. Does not involve meaning words or phrases + visual + understanding.

> **At an Airport:** One can distinguish male, female, old, young voices. Though not understanding what is being said but tone, mannerism, and voice gives some idea.

COMPREHENSIVE LISTENING

Comprehensive Listening involves understanding the message.

> Listener first needs appropriate vocabulary and language skills. Using overly **complicated language or technical jargon**, therefore, can be a barrier to comprehensive listening.

> Comprehensive listening is further complicated by the **fact** that two different people listening to the same thing may understand the message in two different ways.

This problem can be multiplied in a group setting, like a classroom.

These **non-verbal signals can greatly aid communication and comprehension**.

SPECIFIC LISTENING TYPES

Discriminative and comprehensive listening are pre-requisites for specific listening types. Listening types can be defined by the goal of listening.

The three main types most common in interpersonal relationships are I C T : Informational/critical/therapeutic

1. Informational Listening (Listening to Learn)
2. Critical Listening (Listening to Evaluate and Analyse)
3. Therapeutic or Empathetic Listening (Listening to Understand Feelings and Emotions).

In reality you may have more than one goal for listening at any given time. For example, you may be listening to learn whilst also attempting to be empathetic. EMPATHY: The ability to understand and share the feelings of another.

Informational Listening

Whenever you listen to learn something, you are engaged in informational listening.

This is true in many day-to-day situations, in education and at work, when you listen to the news, watch a documentary, when a friend tells you a recipe, or when you are talked through a technical problem with a computer. Like these, there are many other examples of informational listening.

Informational listening, especially in formal settings like in work meetings or while in education, is often accompanied by note-taking: a way of recording key information so that it can be reviewed later. (See 'Note-taking' for more information.)

Critical Listening

We can be said to be engaged in critical listening when the goal is to *evaluate or scrutinize* what is being said. Critical listening is a much more active behaviour than informational listening and usually involves some sort of problem solving or decision making.

Critical listening is akin to critical reading; both involve analysis of the information being received and alignment with what we already know or believe.

Whereas informational listening may be mostly concerned with receiving facts and/or new information, critical listening is about analysing opinion and making a judgment.

When the word 'critical' is used to describe listening, reading, or thinking it does not necessarily mean that you are claiming that the information you are listening to is somehow faulty or flawed. Rather, critical listening means engaging in what you are listening to by asking yourself questions such as: 'what is the speaker trying to say?' or 'what is the main argument being presented?', 'how does what I'm hearing differ from my beliefs, knowledge, or opinion?' Critical listening is, therefore, fundamental to true learning.

It is often important, when listening critically, to have an open mind and not be biased by stereotypes or preconceived ideas. By doing this you will become a better listener and broaden your knowledge and perception of other people and your relationships.

Therapeutic or Empathic Listening

Empathic listening involves attempting to understand the feelings and emotions of the speaker; to put yourself into the speaker's shoes and share their thoughts.

Empathy is not the same as sympathy, it involves more than being compassionate or feeling sorry for somebody else. It involves a deeper connection, a realization and understanding of another person's point of view.

This type of listening does not involve making judgments or offering advice but gently encouraging the speaker to explain and elaborate on their feelings and emotions.

OTHER LISTENING TYPES

Although usually less important or useful in interpersonal relationships there are other types of listening that we engage in:

Appreciative Listening
Appreciative listening is listening for enjoyment. A good example is listening to music, especially as a way to relax.

Rapport Listening
When trying to build rapport with others we can engage in a type of listening that encourages the other person to trust and like us.

Selective Listening
This is a more negative type of listening, it implies that the listener is somehow biased to what they are

hearing. Bias can be based on preconceived ideas or emotionally difficult communications. Selective listening is a sign of failing communication.

GENDER AFFECTS LISTENING ABILITY

Generally, and without trying to stereotype, men and women value communication differently.

Women tend to place a higher value on connection, cooperation, and emotional messages,

Men are generally more concerned with facts and maybe uncomfortable talking about and listening to personal or emotional subjects.

This doesn't mean that women are better listeners than men or vice-versa, but that there may be differences in the ways in which messages are interpreted. During a conversation, men and women are likely to ask different types of questions of the speaker to clarify the message; their final interpretation of the conversation may, therefore, be different.

These words have been passed along in loving memory of ROSE:

Remember, Growing Older is Mandatory, Growing Up is Optional.

We make a Living by what we get. We make a Life by what we give…

God promises a safe landing, not a calm passage. If God brings you to it, He will bring you through it.

Listening with an Open Mind

Step 1

Place yourself in the other person's shoes. It's easy to get lost in yourself and to only consider the impact of the other person's 'telling' on you.

But active listening is blocked by your inward thinking. Instead, you must open out and look at the problems from the other person's perspective; and assume that if you had been in their shoes, you would have seen your way through the problem much faster. By being a good listener this can also help you become better friends with the person by getting to know more about them.

When listening to people, engage in the conversation and make eye contact so they know that you care about what they are saying (even if you don't care, it is still polite to do it). People who listen more are more observant and therefore more thoughtful and have a better understanding of things. Make sure you really are listening and not doing something else. Try to make sure you are completely focused on the person who is talking and not get sidetracked.

Instead of immediately judging the person who is speaking, or coming up with a 'solution' right away, just take time to listen and to look at the situation from the other person's perspective. Think about how you would feel if someone was silently judging you. This will help you truly hear the person instead of forming your own opinions before you truly understand the situation at hand.

Step 2

Avoid comparing the person's experiences with your own. Though you may think that the best thing you can do to really listen is to compare the person's experiences to your own, this is far from the truth. If the person is talking about dealing with a death in the family, you can share some wisdom, but avoid saying, 'That's exactly like how it was with me.' This can come off as offensive or insensitive especially when you compare something really serious to your own less-intense experiences; such as comparing someone's recent divorce with your three-month long relationship may cause discomfort to the person you are talking to. You may think that this is the best way to be helpful and to approach the situation, but this type of thinking is actually reductive and can make the person feel like you're not really listening at all.

Avoid saying 'I' or 'me' a lot. This is a good indicator that you're focusing more on yourself than on the person's situation. Of course, if the person knows that you've had a similar experience, then he or she may actively ask for your opinion. In this case, you can offer it, but be cautious about acting like your experiences are exactly like the other person's. This might seem as though you are just trying to make fake situations to seem helpful.

Step 3

Don't try to help immediately. Some people think that when they're listening they should also have their gears turning to find a quick and easy solution to the person's problem. Instead of this attitude, you should take what the person says at face value and take time to think of a 'solution' when the person is speaking, and provide help only if he or she is really looking for help in this way. If you start frantically thinking of all of the quick fixes for the person's problems then you won't really be listening. Focus on absorbing everything the person is saying to you. Only after that can you really try to help.

Step 4

Sympathize. Show them that you care by nodding at appropriate times so they know are listening. Also says little things such as 'yeah' when the person is talking about something that they want you to agree on (you can tell by the tone of their voice); or 'Wow' when the person talks about a tragedy or something bad done against them. Saying these words shows them that you are not only listening but also paying attention. Say these words at the appropriate times and softly so that you don't come off as overbearing and interrupting. Try to appeal to your sensitive side and comfort the person if in distress. But on the other hand most people do not want to be pitied. So comfort them but don't make yourself seem higher than them.

Little Red Book of Reading and Listening Skills

Step 5

Remember what you've been told. One important part of being a good listener is to actually absorb the information the person has told you. So, if the person is telling you about his problems with his best friend, Jake, and you've never met the guy before, you can at least remember his name so you can refer to him that way, making it seem like you're better acquainted with the situation. If you don't remember any names, details, or important events, then it won't sound like you're listening.

It's okay if you don't have a razor sharp memory. However, if you keep having to stop and ask for clarification or keep forgetting who everyone is, then yeah, you won't come off as a very good listener. You don't have to remember every little detail, but you don't want the person who is speaking to feel like they have to repeat themselves a million times either.

Step 6

Follow up. Another important part of being a good listener is that you go beyond just hearing the person out having a conversation and never thinking about it again. If you really want to show that you care, then you should ask the person about the situation the next time you're alone together, or even send him or her a text or give a phone call to see how the situation is progressing. If it's something serious like an impending divorce, a job search, or even a health complication, then it can be very nice to show that you care by checking in, even when you're not being asked to. Don't be put off, however, if they don't want to follow up, accept their decision but tell them you're always there to support them.

The person who talked to you might be touched that you made the effort to actually think about him or her beyond your conversation and to even check in to see how he or she is faring. This takes your listening skills to the next level.

Of course, there's a difference between following up and nagging the person. If the person talked to you about how she wants to quit her job, you probably don't want to send a text every day asking if she did it yet, or you'll be putting unnecessary pressure on the situation and creating stress instead of helping her out.

Step 7

Know what not to do. Knowing what to avoid when you're trying to be a good listener can be almost as helpful as knowing what to do. If you want the speaker to take you seriously and to think that you are being respectful, then here are some general things to avoid:

- ➢ Don't interrupt when the other person is trying to make a point.
- ➢ Don't interrogate the person. Instead, gently ask questions when it's needed (i.e., between gaps or lulls when the person is not talking).
- ➢ Don't try to change the subject, even if it's a little uncomfortable.

> Avoid saying, 'It's not the end of the world' or 'you'll feel better in the morning'. This just minimizes the person's problems and makes him or her feel bad. Make eye contact with the person so that they realize that you are interested and are listening.

Step 8

Be silent at first. It might sound obvious and trite, but one of the biggest obstacles to listening is resisting the urge to voice impulsive thoughts. Likewise, many people falsely express empathy by sharing their own similar experiences. Both 'gut' responses can be helpful, but they are usually overused and ultimately abused.

Put aside your own needs and wait patiently for the other person to unfold their thoughts at their own pace and in their own way.

Step 9

Reassure the person of your confidentiality. If the person is telling you something private or important then you should make it clear that you're a trustworthy person who can keep their mouth shut. Say that the person can trust you, that whatever is said stays between you two, and that your word is your bond. If the person is unsure of whether or not you can really be trusted, then he or she will be less likely to open up. Also don't force anyone to open up to you as this makes them uncomfortable or angry.

Of course, when you say that what the person says will remain confidential, it should be true, unless there are circumstances that prevent you from keeping it to yourself, such as if the person is suicidal and you're deeply concerned. If you can't actually be trusted in general, though, then you'll never be a good listener.

Step 10

Be encouraging when you do speak. It's important to use empathetic sounding back at appropriate intervals during the conversation so the speaker doesn't feel like you're not listening at all. It's helpful to 'summarize and restate' or 'repeat and encourage' the main points. This will help the conversation seem fluid and will make the speaker less self-conscious about talking. Here's what you should do:

Repeat and encourage: Repeat some things the speaker said and at the same time provide positive feedback as encouragement. For example, you might say, 'I can see that you didn't enjoy having to take the blame. I wouldn't have either.' Go easy with this technique, though. Use the empathetic sound back as a nudge from time to time because if you overwork it, you will come across as patronizing.

Summarize and restate: It is highly useful to summarize your understanding of what the 'teller' has said and to restate it in your own words. This reassures the speaker that you have truly been listening to what he or she is saying and that you 'got it'. It also provides the speaker with an opportunity to correct mistaken assumptions and misconceptions on your part.

Make sure to leave the door wide open with statements like, 'I may be wrong, but...' or 'Correct me if I am wrong...' This technique is especially useful when you find yourself getting frustrated or you sense that your listening focus is wavering.

Step 11

Ask meaningful and empowering questions. Refrain from probing or putting the other person on the defensive. Rather, aim to use questions as a means by which the speaker can begin to reach his or her own conclusions about the issues being raised. This can help the speaker make his or her own conclusions without sounding judgmental or too forceful. Here are some things to keep in mind.

Once you have shown empathetic listening, it is time to move into empowered listening: Re-frame the questions you ask. For example, 'You didn't enjoy having to take the blame. But I cannot understand why you feel blamed rather than merely being asked not to do something that way.'

Wording the question in this manner presents the speaker with a need to respond directly to your lack of grasping something. In the response process, the speaker should begin to move from a more emotional response to a more logical and constructive response.

Step 12

Wait for the person to open up. In the process of encouraging a constructive response an active listener must be ever so patient and let the speaker acquire his or her full flow of thoughts, feelings, and ideas. These may, at first, start as a trickle and the full flow may take a long time to develop. If you press too early and ask too many personal, probing questions, that may actually have the opposite of the intended effect and may make the person feel defensive and reluctant to share any information.

Keep your patience and keep your place in the 'teller's' shoes. It sometimes helps to imagine why the 'teller' has worked into such a situation.

Step 13

Do not interrupt with what you feel or think about the 'telling'. Instead, wait for the other person to ask your opinion before breaking the flow of their discourse. Active listening requires the listener to shelve his or her own opinions temporarily and patiently await appropriate breaks in conversation. When the conversation breaks, provide a summary or an empathetic concurrence.

If you interrupt the person too soon, then he or she will be frustrated and won't fully absorb what you're saying. The person will be eager to finish saying his or her part and you'll be causing a nuisance and a distraction.

Abstain from giving direct advice (unless you're asked for it). Instead, let the individual talk the situation out and find his or her own way. This empowers both the individual and you. It is the course most likely to result in beneficial change and self-understanding for the 'teller' and for you.

Step 14

Reassure the speaker. Whatever the conclusion of the conversation, let the speaker know that you have been happy to listen and to be a sounding board. Make it clear that you are open to further discussion if need be, but that you will not pressurize him or her at all. In addition, reassure the speaker of your intention to keep the discussion confidential. Even if the speaker is in a terrible situation and saying something like, 'It's all going to be okay' seems completely inappropriate, you can still reassure the speaker by saying that you're there to listen and to help.

You can even pat the speaker's hand or knee, put an arm around him or her, or give another reassuring touch. Do whatever is appropriate to the situation. You don't want to overstep your bounds when it comes to touching.

Offer to assist with any solutions if you have the ability, time, and expertise. Do not build up false hopes, though. If the only resource you can provide is to continue to be an active listener, make that very clear. This, in and of itself, is an extremely valuable help.

Step 15

When giving advice remember to make it neutral and not too influenced by your own experiences. Think about what is best for the person in question rather than what you did although this may help.

Step 16

Make eye contact. Eye contact is important when you are listening. If you give your friend the impression you aren't interested and are distracted, they may never open up to you again. When someone is talking to you, focus directly on their eyes so that they will know with certainty that you are absorbing every single word. Even if the topic is not interesting to you, at least respect and truly listen to what the speaker has to say.

Focus your eyes, ears, and your thoughts only on him/her and become a good listener. Don't concentrate on thinking about what you will say next, but instead focus fully on what the other person is saying. (Remember that it's about the person, not you.)

Step 17

Give the speaker your full attention. If you want to be a good listener, then it's important for you to create a conducive physical and mental space. Remove all distractions and confer all of your attention to the person who has something to say to you. Turn off communication devices (including cell phones) and arrange to talk in a place with no distractions. Once you are face to face, calm your mind and pay attention to what the other person is telling. Show them that you are helpful.

Pick a place that is free of distractions or other people who might grab your attention. If you go to a coffee shop, make sure you're focused on the person who is speaking and not the interesting characters who walk in and out of the door.

If you're talking in a public place like a restaurant or a cafe, avoid sitting near a television that's on. Even if you're determined to give the person all of your attention, it can be tempting to take a quick look at the television, especially if your favourite team is playing.

Step 18

Encourage the speaker with body language. Nodding your head will indicate that you understand what the speaker is saying, and will encourage them to continue. Adopting body postures, positions, and movements that are similar to the speaker (mirroring them) will enable them to relax and open up more. Try looking straight into their eyes. Not only does this show you are listening, but also that you are really interested in what they are saying.

Another way to have encouraging body language is to turn your body towards the speaker. If you're turned away from the speaker, then it may look like you're itching to leave. If you cross your legs, for example, cross your legs in the direction facing the speaker instead of away.

Don't cross your arms over your chest. This will make you appear standoffish or skeptical even if you don't actually feel that way.

Listen actively to express your interest. Active listening involves the entire body and face—both yours and that of the speaker. You can be quiet while still making it clear that you are hanging on to every word that the speaker is telling you. Here's how you can make the most of the situation by being an active listener.

Your words: Though you don't have to say, 'Hmm', 'I see', or 'right' every five seconds or it will begin to get annoying, you can throw in an encouraging phrase here and there to show that you're paying attention. If the person whom you are talking to really means something to you, then you will surely pay attention and help them sort out their problem if there is any.

Your expression: Look interested and meet the gaze of the speaker from time to time. Do not overwhelm the speaker by staring intently, but do reflect friendliness and openness to what you are listening to.

Read between the lines: Always be alert for things that have been left unsaid and for cues that can help you gauge the speaker's true feelings. Watch the facial and body expressions of the 'teller' to try to gather all information you can, not just from the words. Imagine what kind of state of mind would have made you acquire such expressions, body language, and volume.

Speak at approximately the same energy level as the other person. This way, they will know that the message is getting through and that there is no need to repeat.

Don't expect them to open up immediately. Be patient and willing to just listen, without giving any advice.

Try to repeat what the other person is saying to confirm the exact meaning. Sometimes words can mean two different things. The best way to confirm and avoid misunderstanding between the conversationalists is to repeat what the other person is saying so that the other person knows you were listening and both of you have the same idea.

Consider their circumstances. If they are sensitive, don't give them 'tough love' advice.

The more difficult listening becomes, the more important it is to listen.

Being a good listener is one of the most important skills if you want to advance your career and build meaningful relationships with people.

Never give out your 'amazing' advice (unless they ask you for it). People just want to be listened to, not be lectured at.

Just because someone talks to you about their problems, it doesn't necessarily mean they want or need you to fix anything. They just want a sounding board sometimes.

Avoid parroting by repeating the sentences word for word. This can be quite annoying.

When you look at the person you are listening to, look into their eyes. This shows that you are 100 per cent focused on them, and not distracted by other things going on. Soften your gaze and avoid staring with looks of disbelief. Be comfortable with what is said insofar as is possible.

People don't listen to understand, they hear to reply. Take that into consideration.

Block out any and all distractions around you. This means turn off your cell phone, and refrain from looking out of the window or fiddling with your pencil.

Imagine that there will be a pop quiz on the subject right after. This will help you hone in and focus on key points and be attentive to details.

Keep in mind that sometimes we need to listen 'between the lines', but there are times when we need to absorb things at face value and go with the flow of the teller's unfolding.

'He understands me,' we say with elation when someone perceptively listens to us. 'Oh, forget it,' we say in frustration when others don't listen or understand. How are you as a listener? What are your beliefs about listening?

INDICATE WHETHER YOU AGREE (A) OR DISAGREE (D) WITH THE FOLLOWING:

1. An effective listener pays attention both to what a person is saying and what she or he is not saying.
   ( )   ( )

2. We can understand another person well even if we don't 'hear' their feelings.
   ( )   ( )

3. I can listen better to my subordinates if we have worked through our expectations of one another.
   ( )   ( )

4. Words fully express what a person feels.
   ( )   ( )

5. We tend to hear things which support our prejudices and not hear things which counteract them.
   ( )   ( )

6. Listening with understanding to another means agreeing with him or her.
   ( )   ( )

7. Persons who listen with understanding run the danger of being changed themselves.
   ( )   ( )

8. Our very natural tendency to evaluate is a help to effective listening.
   ( )   ( )

9. Some things can only be said with the help of the listener.
   ( )   ( )

10. Listening is primarily a word process not a people process.
    ( )   ( )

11. As I listen, I should be aware of my own feelings.
    ( )   ( )

12. It's more important that the other be given a chance to talk than that he or she be understood.
    ( )   ( )

13. Advice giving or dogmatic statements tend to superiorize the one who makes them.
    ( )   ( )

14. Silence is not communicative.

Scoring:

> 'Millions of grains of sand in the world. Why such a lonely beach?'

LISTENING: TWO EXERCISES

Here are two exercises that can improve our listening: the first by showing us humorously how not to listen, the second by underlining the difficulty of fully sharing a thought or feeling.

Exercise: Talkathon

Ask for two volunteers. Have them sit and face each other in front of the rest of the group. The instructions are that both should begin talking simultaneously at the instructor's signal. Each may speak on any topic he or she desires (cricket, football, politics, cinema). But they must maintain eye contact with one another. Gestures are very important. The loser will be the speaker that stops first. It's a ridiculous scene but typical of how we often 'listen'.

Exercise: Listen, Repeat, Reply

Choose a controversial topic. For example, 'Is the quality of life in India improving or declining?' Ask for two volunteers holding contrary views on the issue. Sitting face to face in front of the group they are to conduct a discussion on the topic. The rule for the discussion is this: each must repeat to the other's satisfaction a summary of what the other speaker has said before they themselves may reply. Listen, repeat, reply.

The two speakers are told to begin and the instructor watches and enforces the rule. The instructor may interrupt either speaker from time to time to ask whether the listener is satisfied with the summary that the other has given, whether the listener has caught the thought fully. After the conversation has gone on in this fashion for ten minutes, or after the problems of communicating have become clear, the instructor stops the demonstration by the two volunteers. Groups of three are formed with the remaining members and with one member acting as monitor these groups practice the exercise for twenty or thirty minutes, changing the role of monitor after each ten-minute period. The group is reassembled and the instructor leads a discussion on practices that help or hinder effective communication.

LISTENING SKILLS

We all think we are good listeners but actually very few of us really are. Here are some practices that hopefully will make you one of those people that people love because they are good listeners.

There are four things you should check: (1) eye contact, (2) posture, (3) gestures, and (4) your use of paraphrase.

Eye Contact: What is appropriate here differs from culture to culture but establish contact with the speaker with your eyes. Not to look at the other person is a way of manifesting a lack of interest. Conversely, as written in an Urdu ghazal: Love and affection can be better expressed by the eyes than by words.

Posture: While there is no dictionary of body language, many factors like culture, relationship and situation suggest that we do speak with our bodies. If we sit leaning slightly forward, it is a sign of interest and encourages the speaker to let their thoughts and expressions flow. On the other hand, if we lean back away from the speaker, it often expresses disinterest.

Gestures: Natural gestures as you listen can increase the speaker's sense of being heard and accepted.

Paraphrasing: Paraphrasing is restating the speaker's thought but in fewer words. It adds nothing new, changes no directions, asks no question but summarizes the speaker's thought or feelings and informs how they have been understood.

The Three Yes Exercise

Form pairs, A makes a statement. Then B says, 'You mean...' Once B gets three consecutive yeses, then it is B's turn to make the statement and for A to say, 'You mean...'

Little Red Book of Reading and Listening Skills **89**

MORE THAN MEETS THE EAR

We spend years learning how to read and write but not even a class or two on listening! People think that listening is natural and that they do not have to learn it. It's like breathing. So, at least, some think.

This is sad since listening is primarily responsible for the many problems we have with each other. We speak at an average of 150 words per minute but our mind with its billions of cells can process almost a thousand per minute. Managing this excess brain capacity is the clue to effective listening. Yes, there's much more to listening than meets the ear.

Here are **three simple exercises to sensitize us to better listening.**

A. Getting Attention

Let three persons (A, B, C) sit in adjoining places. A and C should speak to B, trying to get B's undivided attention in any way they wish and as best as they can. A and C should ignore the presence of each other.

B. Telegraphic Conversation

Let two persons (A and B) conduct a conversation on a topic of interest with statements that do not exceed ten words. A 10 paise fine is imposed for each word in excess of ten words.

C. Blind Conversation

The two persons now carry on a conversation with their eyes closed. Topic: 'The quality of life: is it improving or deteriorating?'

Question

What do these experiences tell us about listening?

So You Think Listening is Easy?

When a spaceship returns from the moon, we are filled with wonder. So many gadgets, signals, parts and systems could have gone wrong but did not. Wow!

Two people truly sharing one thought or feeling is no less a wonder. Think of the possible slip-ups in any dialogue:

1. What you mean to say.
2. What you actually say.
3. What the other person hears.
4. What they think they hear.
5. What they want to say in response.
6. What they do say in response.
7. What you think they say, and so on.

Every step of the way there can be a mis-communication, a mis-understanding, a mis-listening. This is because we speak and hear, not only with our lips and ears, but with our whole body and our heart.

Our lips speak, but so do our eyes, hands, legs, posture. A person's lips may say they're not nervous, but their hands may be trembling. A person's lips may say that they are very interested, but their eyes may be looking at their watch. When we get one message from a person's lips and another from their body language or behaviour, messages get confused.

And our ears listen but so do our hearts. Like a radio listener we listen to programmes that please us, but we don't like to hear what displeases us. We select what we like to hear. We filter what we do not like. And the more we want to hear something, the more likely we will.

How to Listen

A prisoner in a dungeon is tapping messages on the wall: 'Is anyone listening?'

'Can anyone hear me?'

His despair arises because of the feeling that no one is listening. The thrill when he hears a tap, the joy when there's a response is unparalleled.

The most neglected art, courtesy and necessity today is listening. If as a friend, supervisor, or teacher you can do more than be a good listener, you will have done much for many. Here are some considerations:

1. Hearing is not listening. Hearing doesn't make communication, listening does.

2. Listening must take place at two levels: the level of words and the level of feeling. We're constantly speaking the language of feelings but rarely listening at that level. If you don't understand how a person feels, you haven't understood them.

3. You can't listen to another unless you're listening to yourself. If you can't hear your own feelings you'll never hear theirs. Without an awareness of your own feelings you'll be sending signals to them that you yourself don't perceive. You cannot communicate with another if your own communication system has broken down.

4. Exploration is one thing, argumentation another. Argumentation is the end of listening.

5. Just avoiding interrupting would be a great leap forward for many.

6. No man is an island. People need people and today, more than ever, people need listening.

7. The first duty of love is to listen. To listen is to understand. To understand is to listen.

SAYING A LOT JUST BY LISTENING

Talking is only one of many ways of sharing. It may be the least effective. A touch, a gesture, a tone, a shrug, a wink, or a smile—these and other signs and symbols are so much more communicative.

In fact even your own silence can communicate so much. How does the saying go: 'If you do not understand my silence, you will not understand my words.'

But perhaps listening says most of all.

Listening to another says:

- 'You are important to me.'
- 'You are worth my time and my attention.'
- 'You are saying something worth hearing.'
- 'You are really an interesting person.'
- 'You are okay.'

Listening is powerful. It is affirmative. Hardly anything is more healing, more calming, more creative, more nourishing, more loving. A decision to listen is really a decision to love. And we all know how powerful love is.

Questions

1. When was the last time that somebody listened to you...really listened?

2. Make a list of persons you know who are really good listeners. How many are they? What do they have in common? What effect do they have on you or others?

   'Even the meanest flower that blows brings thoughts too deep for tears.'

In the Sunshine of Attention

Flowers blossom in the sunlight and people when they are listened to. Try the following exercise when you have a group of people together. You'll learn a lot about listening and about people.

Ask for two volunteers. They are to act as consultants in a discussion. Choose a topic. For example, unemployment or specifically why so many young college graduates are not finding employment. Pick two persons (select two who are good in sports and who will not mind a little laughter at their own expense). Tell them that they will be consultants to the group on this topic. Ask them to leave the room and to wait until they are sent for.

Have ten participants from a discussion Circle, leaving two empty places for the two experts who are to assist them in their discussion. Instruct the group that the point of the exercise is to see the effects of attention and inattention. For this end they are to pay rapt attention to Advisor A and little or no attention to Advisor B. They are not to be rude to Advisor B but all their eye contact, gestures, posture, questions and remarks, attention and appreciation should be exclusively directed at A. Should B intervene, he or she must be given that opportunity but with minimal attention if not disinterest; and then immediately afterwards back goes the attention and interest to Advisor A. Caution the group not to give away the plot by telltale smiles but to be very observant of each Advisor's behaviour. Now call in the Advisors and watch the fun.

Fifteen minutes is usually more than enough to allow the effects of attention and inattention to become clear.

Question

What does this tell us about listening? Is listening just a word process or does it affect behaviour, feelings, and personal growth? Which of the two consultants flowered and which wilted?

THE WORDS AND THE MUSIC

Have you heard a good singer? What is it that turns you on? The words? The music? Both, isn't it? The words and the music.

The same is true of all listening. You must hear the words and the music. Don't just hear my words, hear my music. My music is the way I am experiencing life at any given moment—in other words, my feelings. My feelings are my music. They are, as someone has said, like my fingerprints, the colour of my eyes, the sound of my voice: unique to me and unrepeatable. You'll never understand me if you don't hear my feelings.

Feelings are my music: sometimes lonely, sometimes sad; sometimes anxious, sometimes glad. You'll know who I am by the songs I sing; by my music.

Sharing my feelings will let you know me in a new and deeper way. What's more, you will get to know yourself in a new way and that's what makes us grow; but insights dawn only if you hear the music.

So the next time you hear Nazia Hassan or Talat Mahmood, remind yourself: for all real listening you must clearly hear the words and the music.

How to Talk to a Disturbed Person

All of us, at one time or another, have to deal with people who are severely disturbed, angry, excited or hurt. It may be a worker who feels that he has been done a great injustice; a student who feels she has been deliberately neglected; or a friend whose feelings have been hurt. What such persons have in common is unexpressed feelings.

Feelings that are not expressed at the appropriate moment stay with us. They do not disappear. Feelings are like wire springs: you can push them down, but sooner or later they will spring up and often at the wrong moment.

A person gets mixed up and disturbed because their feelings get mixed up. They do not act straight or think straight because they do not feel straight. Only after such feelings have been released can they think clearly and gain insight into their problem.

So your disturbed friend needs understanding more than anything else. To a disturbed person, advice, evaluation or even encouragement are of limited value. What such a person wants, above all, is to be understood. Perhaps we can help them most merely by listening with understanding.

Do not, however, just listen to their words; listen to their feelings. If you don't hear those, you really haven't listened. Effective listening means picking up signals at two levels: the level of words but, even more importantly, the level of feelings.

The best way to 'talk' to a disturbed person is to listen.

WHEN PEOPLE CONFIDE IN YOU

When your friend confides, 'I've never been so discouraged in my life. I've been searching, searching, searching but am no closer to a job today than I was six months ago.'

Should you say:

    a. You shouldn't be discouraged.

    b. You're going to find something tomorrow.

    c. Nothing to show after all that effort.

When a close friend sadly confides, 'My boss said I'm not working fast enough and that he would have to let me go unless I improve.'

Should you say:

    a. If I were you, I'd work harder.

    b. Don't worry. You can always get another job.

    c. You like your job and would not like to lose it.

When your friend confides, 'Now that my father has died, I am finding it hard to give up Law, return to our village, and take care of the fields and our property.'

Should you say:

a. You ought to be happy to return to the countryside.
b. Yours is one of the prettiest villages in Andhra.
c. You're finding it difficult.

The first two answers in each of these three situations actually constitute a lack of acceptance. They either indicate that you do not want to get involved, or they evaluate rather than accept actual feelings, or they do not take the persons' feelings, and consequently the persons themselves, seriously.

The third response is accepting of the person as they are, as they are experiencing life at that moment—a real sharing. Having their problems understood and reflected but left with them shows them that you have faith in their ability to solve their own problems. They will feel more relaxed, comfortable, more positive about themselves and more apt to listen to and accept others.

The Himalayas are for contemplation, the seaside for meditation, but a human is for understanding. When people confide in you, they don't want an evaluation, analysis, or exhortation, they want understanding. Accept me as I am. Listen to me.

LISTENING AND SOMETIMES CHALLENGING

When people who are troubled in their relationships confide in you, you can help them not only by listening but by responding in ways that challenge them to grow and take responsibility for their problems.

I. First of all, of course, you must listen.
  A. Listen not partially, selectively or interpretatively, but, as we've said, with empathy, real concern, and without any facade.
  B. Listen to:
    1. their words, the content, and even more
    2. their feelings, their 'music'
    3. the reasons they give for their feelings
    4. and note the effects of their feelings on their behaviour—the tone, their posture, whole manner. Their message is there.

II. When you have listened to them fully in this way, and warmly accepted them as they are, then, if you feel that there is some distortion in their perception, rather than leave them to linger in that, real concern or friendship may lead you to challenge them to grow. Distorted perceptions lead to distorted relationships. To help them see a truer, fuller picture, you may ask:

  A. 'How does the other person see it?'
  B. 'Why does the other person act the way he or she does?' 'She acts this way because…' These questions bring the problem in focus.

C. Self-defeating attitudes may be seen in the other person. For example, 'I'm no good': in that case reassurance is needed. 'Do you like yourself this way?' 'Do you want to change?' Don't advise; just question with warmth. People will only change if they want to but your questions may help them see their part in the problem's creation and set goals to solve it. That's growth, that's friendship.

'A friend is someone who leaves you with all your freedom intact but who, by what he thinks of you, obliges you to be fully what you are.'

LISTENING AND REDUCING CONFLICT

How often we get into needless conflict just because we do not listen! We will never avoid conflict completely but at least we can avoid conflict which is the result of poor listening. Look at the sets of opinions given below and do the exercise described on the next pages.

A. I believe a child needs firm discipline, including a spanking, when necessary, or...

   I believe you should never hit a child

B. I believe we must trust our neighbouring countries in some way to have peace in the subcontinent, or...

   I believe we cannot trust these countries.

C. I believe the reservation policy (jobs, promotions) should continue or...

   I believe the policy should not continue.

D. I believe the man as head of the family should make the major decisions in the family, or…

   I believe marriage is an equal partnership and both the man and woman should agree on major decisions.

E. I believe that hospital employees should have the right to strike, or…

   I believe hospital employees should not have the right to strike.

F. I believe the language formula should be English and the mother tongue, or…

   I believe the language formula should not be English and the mother tongue.

G. I believe the death penalty is sometimes a necessary and just punishment, or…

   I believe the death penalty is always unjust.

H. I believe a woman has a right to have an abortion if she wishes to, or…

   I believe a woman has no right to have an abortion.

Exercise

Step 1:   Form pairs.

Step 2:   Choose one set of statements on the preceding page over which the two of you disagree.

Step 3:   Each writes their belief and all the reasons and supporting evidence for it.

Belief:

Reasons:

1.

2.

3.

4.

Step 4: Each should read their belief statement and the supporting reasons while the other listens attentively but with no argumentation. Then the other reads while the first listens. Again clarifications only.

Step 5: When both have been heard, each writes down any points of the other person with which he or she agreed.

Points I heard my partner say with which I agree.

1.

2.

3.

Step 6: Share these points with your partner.

Step 7: Answer the following questions:

a. Did you feel listened to during the exercise?

b. Did anything surprise you?

c. Did you learn anything?

Step 8: Share your responses with your partner.